"I WANT TO ENTERTAIN PEOPLE. THAT'S MY WHOLE LIFE—TO MY LAST BREATH."

ELVIS PRESLEY

1935–1977

ABDO
Publishing Company

Lives Cut Short

Elvis Presley

Rock & Roll's King

By Stephanie Watson

Credits

Published by ABDO Publishing Company, PO Box 398166, Minneapolis, MN 55439.

Printed in the United States of America,
North Mankato, Minnesota
062012
092012

 THIS BOOK CONTAINS AT LEAST 10% RECYCLED MATERIALS.

Editor: Rebecca Felix
Series Designer: Becky Daum

Library of Congress Cataloging-in-Publication Data
Watson, Stephanie.
Elvis Presley : rock & roll's king / by Stephanie Watson.
p. cm. -- (Lives cut short)
Includes bibliographical references.
ISBN 978-1-61783-482-0
1. Presley, Elvis, 1935-1977--Juvenile literature. 2. Rock musicians--United States--Biography--Juvenile literature. I. Title.
ML3930.P73W37 2012
782.42166092--dc23
[B]

2012001288

Table of Contents

1

Shaking Up Variety Shows

In 1956, Elvis Presley was the hottest singer in the United States. His songs "Hound Dog," "Don't Be Cruel," and "Blue Suede Shoes" were burning their way up the charts. Despite that fact, popular television variety show host Ed Sullivan swore he would never have Presley on his family-oriented show.

Although he was all the rage socially and musically, Presley was also the most controversial singer in the industry. When he performed, he did not just stand on a stage and sing into

▸ Elvis Presley's music and moves caused a stir in the 1950s.

a microphone. His whole body moved to the rhythm of the music. He pumped his hips and wiggled his legs. He threw his arms in the air and curled his upper lip seductively. Today, his moves would be considered pretty mild. But at the time, they were radically new. They were so scandalous they earned him the nickname "Elvis the Pelvis."

On June 5, 1956, Presley sang and danced his way through his hit "Hound Dog" during his second appearance on *The Milton Berle Show*. The episode shocked some viewers. It also earned Berle his highest ratings ever. Approximately one month later, Presley sent *The Steve Allen Show*'s ratings soaring, too. There

The Ed Sullivan Show

If Presley changed the course of popular music, the same can be said about Sullivan and the course of television. His entertainment variety show aired for 23 years—from 1948 to 1971—holding the record for longest-running primetime live entertainment show in the history of US television. It was a family show with something for everyone, and it was widely popular with viewers of all ages. The show helped launch some of the biggest musical acts of the twentieth century, including Presley with his memorable performances, the Beatles, the Rolling Stones, and the Jackson Five, as well as numerous comedians.

Sullivan was a former radio-show host and emcee. He had no performance talent of his own, but had a knack for spotting talent in others. Sullivan booked enough talented musicians and comedians to make his show a hit—and to make himself a big star.

was no denying audiences loved Presley.

As much as Sullivan disliked Presley's antics, he hated even more the idea of his television rivals beating him in ratings. So, finally, he reluctantly signed Presley to do three episodes of his show.

On September 9, 1956, Presley made his first appearance on *The Ed Sullivan Show*. He opened with his latest hit, "Don't Be Cruel." Then he slowed things down with the ballad "Love Me Tender." The girls in the audience shrieked and swooned as Presley sang and did his signature moves. Presley performed two more songs: "Hound Dog" and "Ready Teddy."

By the end of the episode, Presley earned Sullivan his highest ratings ever and broke television viewing records. Sixty million people watched the show—more than 80 percent of US television households at the time.

Sullivan Pays Presley a Fortune

Sullivan agreed to pay Presley an unheard-of fee for his 1956 appearances—$50,000 for three shows. At the time, huge stars such as actor Bing Crosby and singer Frank Sinatra were only making approximately $7,500 per television appearance.

The King

Audiences were fascinated by Presley's sound. Blending rhythm and blues (R&B), country, and gospel like no one had before him, Presley had

▲ Presley's style and sound had a major impact on his generation and made him an eternal icon.

created something entirely new. He helped give birth to rock and roll. "The people were looking for something different and I came along just in time. I was lucky," Presley said.[1]

Every time Presley performed, he nearly created a riot. Girls shrieked, fainted, and stampeded the stage just to touch and kiss him.

Presley's music, moves, and image became iconic. As of 2012, Presley had sold more than 1 billion records worldwide. Nearly 150 of his songs made it into the *Billboard* Top 100 chart, and 18 of them had shot all the way to Number 1. One hundred and fifty of his albums went gold (500,000 copies sold) or platinum

(1 million copies sold). And he starred in more than 30 successful movies.

> "In cultural terms, his coming was nothing less than the start of a revolution."[2]
>
> *—Historian David Halberstam commenting on the start of Presley's career*

Presley also sparked controversy in a way no artist before him had done. Decades before Britney Spears shaved her head or Lady Gaga wore a dress made from meat, Presley's sexy, hip-shaking moves shocked many Americans. Parents, preachers, and politicians accused him of corrupting the country's youth. Whether people loved him or hated him, they could not deny his popularity. Ultimately, Presley would come to reign over the rock-and-roll world.

Presley's bright career ended too soon with his sudden death at age 42, but his legend has proven immortal. Today, fans celebrate his life and commemorate the anniversary of his death. They collect his records and watch his movies over and over again. To the music world and fans alike, Presley is considered a musical legend and leader, which is why he was and is evermore called "the King." It is not clear who first gave him the title, but it reflects his position at the top of the rock-and-roll industry.

2

Born in a Shotgun Shack

The man who would be known as the King came from far humbler beginnings. Elvis was the child of Vernon and Gladys Presley, sharecroppers who worked other farmers' land in exchange for a percentage of the crops. The couple was so poor when they married in 1933 that 17-year-old Vernon had to borrow the three dollars needed to buy a marriage license.

Vernon and Gladys fell hard for each other when they met at Roy Martin's grocery store in Tupelo, Mississippi. Vernon was blond haired,

▸ Elvis with his parents, Gladys and Vernon Presley, in 1938

blue-eyed, and charming. Gladys inherited her dark hair and exotic looks from her Cherokee ancestors. In addition to good looks, Gladys had distinctive dance moves. She was known for her buck dancing—a hip-swinging, foot-stomping type of rhythm—a talent Elvis likely inherited.

On January 8, 1935, at 4:35 a.m., Gladys gave birth to a son whom the couple named Elvis Aaron Presley. Elvis was Vernon's middle name.

Elvis spent his early years in a Tupelo shack that Vernon had built with his brother, Vester. When Elvis was a baby, his mother carried him in a sack she wore as she picked cotton. To pass the long, backbreaking hours, the African American workers around them sang a mix of gospel, blues, and old African chants. Those songs were Elvis's lullabies, and elements of this African-American music would show up in his own music later in life.

Elvis's Twin

Elvis was not Gladys and Vernon's only child. He had a twin brother, Jesse Garon, who was stillborn. Jesse was buried in an unmarked grave at Priceville Baptist Church and Cemetery in Tupelo; his parents could not afford $3.50 for a headstone. Years later, Elvis built a marker at his Graceland mansion to honor the memory of his lost twin.

Throughout his life, Elvis felt guilty he survived while Jesse died. He was plagued by thoughts that, somehow, he had not done enough to protect his twin in their mother's womb. Losing her firstborn made Gladys especially protective and proud of Elvis.

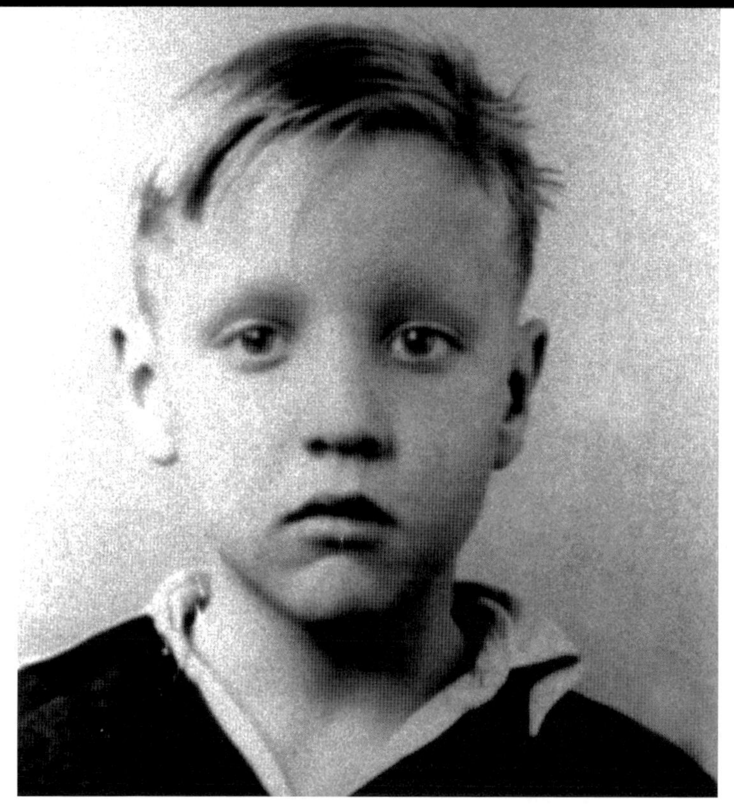

▲ The Presleys' finances were lean for much of Elvis's early life.

Vernon Goes to Prison

In 1937, times were tough for Vernon. He was barely making ends meet as a sharecropper and working odd jobs. So when his brother-in-law and a friend suggested adding more money to the amount on a four-dollar check Vernon received for the sale of a hog, he agreed.

The men were quickly arrested and charged with forgery. Vernon was sent to the state penitentiary in Parchman, Mississippi, to serve out a three-year sentence. Two-year-old Elvis and his mother were left alone.

Without Vernon's income, the Presleys could not afford to pay for their tiny home, and it was repossessed. Gladys and Elvis went to live with her cousins, Frank and Leona Richards, in South Tupelo. Gladys got a job working at the nearby Mid-South Laundry. Every weekend, she and Elvis traveled for five hours by bus to visit Vernon.

Elvis and his mother grew especially close during this time. They developed their own special language that no one else understood. For example, their word for ice cream was "iddytream." Elvis nicknamed his mom "Satnin," which roughly meant "to fatten

Elvis's Birthplace

Today, visitors to Tupelo, Mississippi, can tour the tiny shack where Elvis was born and spent his early years. It was what is referred to as a *shotgun shack*. The term is used to describe a house so small and squat that a bullet fired from a shotgun through the front door would whiz straight through the back door without hitting anything in between.

Although some elements have been replaced and restored, the house remains in the spot it was built. The tourist attraction includes a memorial garden and a "walk of life"—42 granite blocks, each one representing a year of Elvis's life.[1] There is even a 1939 green Plymouth—a replica of the car the Presleys owned in the 1940s—and a restored Assembly of God Church where Elvis used to attend services with his parents.

up." In return, Gladys called him "Elvie" or "Naughty."[2]

Elvis Finds His Voice

Vernon was released from prison after just eight months for good behavior, but the tough times continued for the Presley family. It was the middle of the Great Depression, a severe worldwide economic slump. As an ex-con with little schooling, Vernon could only find odd jobs here and there. Meanwhile, Gladys picked cotton. Between the two of them, they could barely afford to feed their growing boy.

During his difficult early years, music became Elvis's escape. He had always enjoyed listening to the joyful gospel music when the family went to church on Sundays. When Elvis was just two years old, he jumped from his mother's lap and rushed up to sing with the choir. He could not yet pronounce the words, but he could mimic the melodies. In the mornings at elementary school, Elvis sang with his class. "Even then, he would sing with such meaning. Some of us actually swelled up with tears," recalled a classmate.[3]

In the segregated South, music was African American or white. But Elvis loved both. He listened to R&B and gospel in Tupelo's African-American Shake Rag neighborhood. And he tuned in to country on the Grand Ole Opry radio show.

On October 3, 1945, ten-year-old Elvis entered a contest at the Mississippi-Alabama Fair and Dairy Show at the Tupelo Fairgrounds. Singing one of his favorite songs, "Ole Shep," about a boy whose dog died, Elvis won over the crowd of 200 people. He came in fifth place, earning him five dollars in ride tickets.

For his next birthday, Elvis's parents bought him a $12.95 guitar from the Tupelo Hardware Company. Elvis learned to play a few chords. He started bringing his guitar to school, telling his classmates that one day he was going to make it onto the Grand Ole Opry show. They laughed at his lofty dreams.

Segregation in the South

Elvis grew up in the South during the 1940s—a time when segregation was the law. African-American and white people were strictly separated. They could not go to the same schools, eat at the same restaurants, or even use the same bathrooms.

Music was also sharply divided during this time. African-American people had jazz and blues, while white people had pop and country music. Elvis was revolutionary for blending the music of both races into his own unique sound.

Moving to Memphis

In the fall of 1948, Vernon was frustrated because he could not find work in Tupelo. On November 6, he packed up his family's belongings in their 1939 Plymouth car and they moved to Memphis, Tennessee.

▲ Elvis wanted a rifle or a bicycle for his eleventh birthday, but Gladys persuaded him to get a guitar instead.

The Presleys lived in a single room of a run-down boardinghouse for a few months and then moved into a public housing project called Lauderdale Courts. Vernon got a job at a local paint company stacking cans for 83¢ an hour.

Elvis was not interested much in his classes or in his classmates at Memphis's Humes High School. He was shy and kept to himself. His grades were mediocre. He was not interested in playing sports. Only one thing captured his attention, and that was music. Very quickly, he picked up on the vibrant Memphis music scene. He especially liked disc jockey (DJ) Dewey Phillips of WHBQ 560 radio. Phillips's *Red, Hot & Blue* show was radical for its time because he played both African-American and white music—a blend of blues, gospel, R&B, and country.

Elvis started hanging out on Beale Street, the heart of the Memphis music scene. The street was packed with record shops and jazz clubs. He started buying brightly colored shirts and dress pants at the ultra-hip Lansky Brothers' clothing store, where all the musicians shopped. He grew his blond hair long and slicked it back. Elvis did not look anything like the other kids at his high school, but that did not matter to him. He wanted to stand out.

On June 3, 1953, Elvis graduated from high school. College was not even a possibility—the family was too poor to afford tuition. Elvis worked odd jobs at a machinist's shop and on an assembly line. He got a job driving a truck for the Crown Electric Company, making approximately $35 a week.

Family Features

Blond haired, blue-eyed Elvis inherited his father's coloring and hints of both his parents' good looks. His hair grew darker as he got older, and he eventually dyed it black.

▲ Although he was shy, Elvis played guitar in a student talent show at Humes High School. He won and even performed an encore.

He said he wanted to become an electrician, but inside he knew music was his true calling. When he was not working, Elvis strummed his guitar, dreaming of the day he would become a famous singer. He just needed his big break.

3

Sun Studio Spark

It was a sweltering, sticky summer afternoon in 1953 when Presley walked into a red brick building known as Sun Studio in downtown Memphis. The studio was officially named the Memphis Recording Service and was the home of the label Sun Records. Launched in 1952, Sun Records belonged to music producer Sam Phillips, who by then had become legendary. Phillips knew how to spot talent. He had recorded with blues greats such as B. B. King, Howlin' Wolf, Rufus Thomas, and Junior Parker.

▸ Sun Studio in Memphis, Tennessee

SUN
Studio
SUN
Studio
ELVIS PRESLEY
AND SUN RECORDS

Phillips had trouble, however, getting white audiences to listen to these African-American musicians in the still-segregated South. He told his secretary, Marion Keisker, "If I could find a white man who had the Negro sound and the Negro feel, I could make a billion dollars."[1]

Keisker was on the lookout for that billion-dollar sound. On this particular July day, Presley walked through the door. Anyone could go to Sun Records' Memphis Recording Service and pay to have a song recorded. The studio's motto was, "We Record Anything, Anywhere, Anytime."[2] Presley told Keisker he was there simply because he wanted to record a song as a present for his mother's birthday. Yet Gladys's birthday had passed two months earlier. Presley was really there to try to get notorious producer Phillips to hear his voice.

Phillips was not in that afternoon, however, so Keisker had to make the recording. She asked, "Who do you sound like?"[3] In a soft, shy voice Presley replied, "I don't sound like nobody."[4]

He began to sing a ballad called "My Happiness." Then he recorded a second song for the album, "That's When Your Heartaches Begin." Presley paid his $3.98 recording fee. Keisker gave him his record, but she also kept

▲ Phillips, *far right*, Presley, *far left*, with bass player Bill Black, *middle left*, and guitarist Scotty Moore, *middle right*, at Sun Studios

a copy. She wrote a note to go with it: "Good ballad singer. Hold."[5]

"That's All Right (Mama)"

In January 1954, Presley returned to record another album at Sun Records. This time, Phillips was there. He listened as Presley recorded two more ballads. He liked what he heard—he just did not have the right song for Presley's voice. Phillips promised to call if he found the right song for them to record together.

During the next few months, Presley was like a shadow at Sun Records, asking Phillips again and again if he had found a song for him. The answer was always no. Finally, in June, Phillips thought he found a song—a ballad called "Without You." Phillips recorded take after take of Presley singing the song, but it just did not sound right in Presley's voice.

Phillips then connected Presley with two local musicians—guitarist Scotty Moore and bassist Bill Black. On July 5, the three men went into the recording studio together. First they tried a few ballads, but Phillips still was not sold. He asked, "Elvis, ain't there something you know that you can sing?"[6] Presley thought about it. Then, he and the two musicians launched into a blues number by Arthur "Big Boy" Crudup called "That's All Right (Mama)." Only, this was not the song the way Crudup had sung it. This was faster. Presley's version blended sounds traditionally associated with both African-American and white music, with hints of blues, gospel, and country. Phillips knew music, but this take on the song was like nothing he had ever heard. He said it felt "like someone stuck me in the rear end with a brand-new super sharp pitchfork."[7] Phillips had found his billion-dollar singer.

PLAY IT AGAIN, DEWEY

Phillips was so excited about the record he immediately brought it to his friend DJ Dewey Phillips (no relation). He knew if he could get Dewey to play the song, it was sure to be a hit.

On July 8, 1954, just days after "That's All Right" was recorded, Dewey premiered it on his *Red, Hot & Blue* radio show. At around 9:30 p.m., Dewey put Presley's record on his turntable. Almost as soon as the record started spinning, the phones at the radio station began ringing. Listeners were fascinated—"That's All Right" was unlike anything they had heard before.

While his song was catching the ears of the Memphis radio audience, Presley was hiding out in a movie theater, fearful everyone would laugh at his song. When Dewey called Gladys and Vernon and insisted Presley do an immediate

What Do You Call That Music?

The music Presley and his band started playing in 1954 did not yet have a name. The mix of R&B, country, and spiritual music came out of the young musicians' own experiences. Some called it *race music*, because it sounded similar to the songs African-American musicians were playing. Others called it *bopping hillbilly* (later referred to as *rockabilly*) for its blend of country and up-tempo beats. "Scotty was coming out of a jazz and country thing, I liked Western swing, and I don't know where the people got the term 'rock 'n' roll' to describe us," drummer D. J. Fontana (who joined Presley's band in 1955) said years later. "For us, that sound came naturally because it's what we'd been playing all our lives."[8]

on-air interview, they had to track him down and bring him into the radio station. He was so shy that Dewey did the entire interview without telling Presley he had switched on the microphone.

The audience had assumed Presley was African American based on the type of music he was singing. During the interview, they discovered he was actually white. Without realizing it or meaning to, Presley had broken a racial barrier.

Phillips hustled Presley back into the studio to record "Blue Moon of Kentucky" for the "B" side of "That's All Right." The single was released on July 19, 1954. Sun Records immediately received 6,000 orders. White people were buying the single. African-American people were buying it. Yet no one knew what to call Presley's sound.

Two-Sided Record Albums

Records are played on a machine called a record player, which turns a record at a constant speed as a mechanical arm runs along the record's surface to produce vibrations. Grooves in the record produce varying vibrations, resulting in sound. When records were first invented in the late nineteenth century, they had music on only one side. That changed with the introduction of the double-sided record in the early twentieth century.

By the 1950s, record companies were releasing songs on records called 45s—seven-inch records that played at a speed of 45 revolutions per minute (RPM). On the "A" side was the song that the record company hoped would get played on the radio and become a hit. The "B" side held an additional track.

▲ PRESLEY WAS NERVOUS PLAYING HIS FIRST FEW LIVE PERFORMANCES WITH ELVIS AND THE BLUE MOON BOYS, BUT AUDIENCES WENT WILD FOR HIM.

Whatever Presley was playing, it was totally new—and people loved it.

SHAKE, RATTLE, AND ROLL

Presley, Moore, and Black started playing small clubs in the Memphis area as Elvis and the Blue Moon Boys. On July 30, 1954, less than two weeks after his record hit stores, Presley and his band performed their first big concert. They opened for country music great Slim Whitman at the Overton Park band shell in Memphis.

When Presley walked onstage in front of that huge audience, he was shaking so badly he had to raise himself up on the balls of his feet just to steady his legs. Watching him move, the girls in the audience started screaming. At first, Presley thought they were making fun of him. "The first time that I appeared on stage, it scared me to death. I really didn't know what all the yelling was about," Presley recalled in

First Love and Fame

In high school, Presley did not have much luck with girls. He was awkward and shy—a shadow of the ladies' man he would one day become.

In January 1954, just before he recorded his first single, 19-year-old Presley noticed pretty, petite brunette Dixie Locke at his family's church. Dixie was a sophomore in high school. And she noticed Presley, too. "My girlfriends and I, we had all . . . kind of had our eye on him and was wondering how we were going to meet him," Dixie said.[9] She and her girlfriends got together a plan. At church one day, they gathered within earshot of Presley and discussed their plans to go roller-skating the following weekend, hoping he might hear and show up. He did. At the local Rainbow roller-skating rink, Dixie finally got the nerve to go up to Presley and introduce herself.

Dixie and Presley began an old-fashioned courtship. Eventually, Presley gave her a ring. They talked about getting married. But as Presley's fame grew, so did his interest in other women. Eventually, Dixie got tired of waiting, and they broke up.

a 1972 interview. As his legs twitched more, the screaming grew louder. When he went backstage, he asked the stage manager, "What'd I do? What'd I do?" The manager replied, "Whatever it is, go back and do it again."[10]

Presley did do it again. The more he played, the more confident he became. And the more the girls screamed, the more he teased them with his shaking hips and sultry smile. Said friend Jerry Schilling,

> *Those crazy legs shook and trembled, his arms pinwheeled, he tossed his body around like he was nothing more than a rag doll with a great head of ducktails. . . . His moves were more outrageous than anything I'd ever seen or heard of, but they were also perfectly timed and executed.*[11]

Elvis and the Blue Moon Boys continued to tour, playing local clubs and gaining popularity. On October 2, Presley finally had the chance to perform at the venue where he had once promised his classmates he would play—the Grand Ole Opry in Nashville, Tennessee.

Grand Ole Opry

The Grand Ole Opry, or the Opry, located in Nashville, has been called "country's most famous stage."[12] Its radio show started broadcasting in 1925. Since then, the Opry stage has hosted some of the biggest acts in country music, including Loretta Lynn, Garth Brooks, Dolly Parton, and Trisha Yearwood.

The response to his performance was not what he had imagined, though. Used to watching country acts, the audience gave Presley a chilly reception. The show's talent coordinator even suggested he go back to driving a truck. Presley did not take the suggestion. Instead, he finally quit his job at Crown Electric to pursue his music career full-time.

Presley could afford to quit because he and his band had finally gotten a regular gig—playing for a weekly country music radio show called *Louisiana Hayride. Louisiana Hayride* broadcast live from Shreveport, Louisiana, to almost 200 radio stations in 13 states. This show's audience did not seem to mind that Presley was not a country singer. In fact, the audience would sometimes go into a frenzy clamoring to be near him. In an effort to calm the crowd after a performance, emcee Horace Lee Logan said, "Elvis has left the building."[13] The phrase caught on and was used by many announcers during Presley's shows throughout his career.

During the rest of each week, Elvis and the Blue Moon Boys traveled across the South playing in clubs. Between 1954 and the spring of 1955, the band clocked more than 25,000 miles (40,234 km) traveling for performances. Presley

▲ ALREADY A BLAZING SUCCESS IN THE SOUTH, PRESLEY WAS ON THE BRINK OF NATIONAL SUPERSTARDOM BY 1955.

was starting to make a name for himself, but it would take a man who was truly larger than life to push him to the brink of superstardom.

4

Colonel's Control

While Presley spread his music throughout the South, Memphis DJ Bob Neal managed the business end of his career. Neal had booked Presley for the Overton Park concert. Afterward, he called Phillips and asked if Presley had a manager. Presley did not at the time, so Neal took over and was later signed on as manager in January 1955.

At the same time, someone else was waiting in the wings, keeping a close watch on Presley's career. It was "Colonel" Thomas A. Parker,

▸ "Colonel" Thomas Parker and Presley in 1957

a promoter who was already managing some popular country singers. Parker was not a real military colonel, although he had served in the army. Louisiana governor Jimmie Davis had given Parker the honorary title for reasons unknown—and he used the title to make himself seem more important.

Parker was determined to become Presley's manager. He knew Presley was destined to become a huge star, and he wanted to be the person who took him to the top. By February 1955, Parker was doing everything he could to convince the young singer and his parents to let him take over for Neal. But Gladys did not trust Parker's

Who Was the Real "Colonel" Parker?

Some people thought Parker was a genius, considering he led Presley to one of the most successful careers in music history. Others thought he was little more than a con man. Yet few people knew the real Parker.

Although many people who met him assumed he was American, Parker was actually born Andreas Cornelis van Kuijk in Breda, Holland. As a teenager, he ran away from home and stowed away on an ocean liner headed for the United States. He enlisted in the US Army to try to gain citizenship. Although he did not go through the naturalization process to become a US citizen, he could enlist as a foreign national legally residing in the country. He changed his name to Thomas A. Parker, after his commanding officer. He worked a variety of odd jobs until finding his place in music management—and meeting Presley.

▲ Parker was a big guy and had a big personality. He often smoked cigars and wore odd hats.

smooth sales pitch. She called him a "fast-talking bullshooter."[1]

Parker wined and dined the Presleys, taking them to dinner at the swanky Peabody Hotel in Memphis. Finally, in August 1955, he persuaded Presley to sign a management contract. Parker immediately took over most of the decisions about Presley's career. Neal's contract with Presley was not set to expire until the following March, so he stayed involved as an advisor. Inexperienced in the ways of the music industry, the Presleys did not realize what was in the fine print of the contract with Parker. Parker had given himself a hefty 25 percent cut of everything Presley earned (an agent normally gets approximately 10 percent of an artist's earnings), plus expenses. Later, Parker reportedly bragged about how he had "suckered the Presleys."[2]

Presley did not feel suckered at the time. In fact, he was grateful to have the experienced Parker take him under his wing. He sent Parker a telegram that read, "Believe me when I say I will stick with you through thick and thin and do everything I can to uphold your faith in me."[3]

On November 21, Parker brokered a deal for Phillips to sell Presley's Sun Records contract to a bigger studio—RCA Records. It may seem odd that Phillips would give up his most profitable new talent, but he needed the money to keep struggling Sun Records afloat. The $35,000 Phillips received for Presley's contract was a huge sum at

"Million Dollar Quartet"

In 1955, Presley ended his recording contract with Sun Records, but he would return to the studio that discovered him for one last, historic recording session. On December 4, 1956, Presley joined three other legendary musicians—Carl Perkins, Jerry Lee Lewis, and Johnny Cash—for an impromptu jam session. The quartet performed a medley of gospel, country, and blues songs. A reporter from the *Memphis Press Scimitar* who was listening in on the session dubbed the group the "Million Dollar Quartet."[4] The four singers never performed together again, but the event became legendary and even spawned the 2010 Broadway musical, *Million Dollar Quartet*.

the time. The contract sale also gave Presley a large sum: he got a $5,000 advance, which was comparable to more than $40,000 today and was probably more money than Presley had ever seen in his life.

Presley finally had enough money to buy things that had been out of reach. He bought himself a pink-and-black Cadillac car. For his parents, Presley bought a brand-new, four-bedroom house in an upscale section of Memphis. It was a big improvement from the public housing project where the family had been living.

New-Home Hubbub

Buying his parents a home had an unexpected effect. Once Presley's fans found out he was living there too, they showed up in droves. Some girls climbed into Presley's bedroom windows at the Audubon Drive home. Others camped out on the lawn. Ever the loving mother, Gladys brought them cake and soda while they waited for Presley to come home.

"Heartbreak Hotel"

On January 10, 1956, Presley did his first recording session in RCA's Nashville studio. His first single, "Heartbreak Hotel," was based on a newspaper story about a suicide that featured the line, "I walk a lonely street."[5] The songwriters wrote it in just 20 minutes, and one vowed it would be Presley's first million-selling record. They were right. "Heartbreak Hotel" went on to sell more than 1 million copies, earning Presley

▲ PRESLEY HOLDING HIS FIRST GOLD RECORD, AWARDED FOR "HEARTBREAK HOTEL"

his first gold record on April 14. It stayed at Number 1 for eight weeks and was rated the Number 1 single of 1956 by *Billboard*.

Presley would claim five spots in the *Billboard* Top 20 of 1956. In addition to "Heartbreak Hotel," he topped the charts with "Don't Be Cruel," "Hound Dog," "I Want You, I Need You, I Love You," and "Love Me Tender." His first album, *Elvis Presley*, sold 1 million copies. The April 30 issue of *LIFE* magazine proclaimed Presley "A Howling Hillbilly Success" who "overnight [became] the biggest singing attraction for teen-agers in the U.S."[6]

Rock and Roll's Roots

Rock-and-roll music became popular during the mid-1950s, and Presley was one of its greatest innovators. Rock's roots go as far back as the 1920s, though. Its sound was forged from a blend of pop, country and western, and R&B. Many early rock-and-roll stars were R&B crossover artists. Presley made his mark by combining white and African-American sounds, which made rock and roll appeal to a much wider audience.

Rock and roll was taking over the US music scene. And although Presley had not invented it, he certainly had a hand in influencing its sound.

5

ELVIS FEVER SPREADS

Presley's career was on fire. He was on the verge of becoming a megastar—but he was not quite there yet. Parker knew to truly make Presley a household name, he had to get the rising star on television.

In the mid-1950s, television was entering a boom period. Just a decade earlier, only 2 percent of Americans had access to a television. By 1954, more than 50 percent had a television set in their homes. Families spent an average of six hours a

▸ SINGING WITH HIS EYES CLOSED, HIPS SWIVELING, AND LIPS CURLED FELT NATURAL FOR PRESLEY, BUT IT WAS INTERPRETED AS SENSUAL—OR EXPLICIT—BY MANY.

day watching sitcoms, news, and entertainment variety shows.

Parker wanted to book Presley to perform on one of those popular variety shows. He sent Jackie Gleason, the producer of *Stage Show*, a glossy photo of Presley. On the back he wrote a note—"JG: This is Elvis Presley. About to be Real Big . . . Colonel."[1]

The note worked. Presley made his television debut on *Stage Show* on January 28, 1956. Presley sang "Shake, Rattle and Roll." Gleason was sold. He signed Presley on for five more appearances.

Next, Parker booked Presley on another variety show, *The Milton Berle Show*. His first appearance on the show was on April 3, but it was his second appearance that earned Berle his highest ratings ever.

Performing on television for a national audience was just the publicity boost Presley needed to become a megastar. With publicity, however, came controversy. Now that they could see Presley, critics were outraged by his moves, which they considered obscene. Presley swore he did not mean to be offensive. "When I sing this rock 'n' roll, my eyes won't stay open and my legs won't stand still. I don't care what they say, it ain't nasty," he vowed.[2]

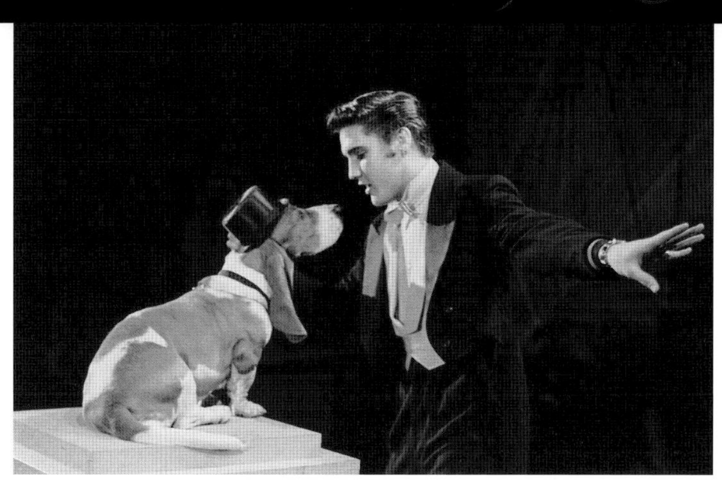

▲ PRESLEY'S SUBDUED PERFORMANCE ON *THE STEVE ALLEN SHOW*, JULY 1, 1956

The controversy over Presley's moves reached its peak on July 1, 1956. Presley was slated to appear on *The Steve Allen Show*. Allen was not a fan. He hated rock-and-roll music. Several citizens' groups urged Allen to cancel Presley, but he refused. He knew what kind of ratings Presley could bring to his show. Instead, Allen toned down Presley's moves.

Presley came out dressed in a tux and sang a mellow version of "Hound Dog" to an actual hound dog—a basset hound wearing a bow tie and a top hat. This time there were no gyrating hips or thrusting pelvis. Presley did not like the performance. Neither did his teenage fans. Allen was happy, though. He had managed to make Presley family friendly and beat his primetime rival *The Ed Sullivan Show* in ratings. But Sullivan was about to one-up Allen.

Presley appeared on *The Ed Sullivan Show* on September 9, 1956. The performance broke ratings records and became the highlight of Presley's television appearances. That first performance was followed up by the additional two appearances on the show Sullivan had booked him for. Presley's last *Sullivan* performance was on January 6, 1957. The television network was trying to present a more wholesome Presley. While Presley performed, he was shot only from the waist up, leaving his swiveling hips off camera. At the end of the show, Sullivan—the man who once swore he would never have Presley on his show—proved he had changed his opinion about the singer. He told the audience, "I wanted to say to Elvis Presley and the country that this is a real decent, fine boy."[3]

As critics attacked Presley's moves, ministers and lawmakers condemned his music. At the time, many public figures charged that rock and roll was corrupting America's youth. Because Presley was such a popular star, these allegations were often aimed at him. The conflict over rock and roll created a generational gap. Most teenagers loved it. Many parents and other adults hated it in the beginning. Some towns even banned public places from playing songs by Presley and other popular rock artists. Whether his music was banned or adored, his moves making waves or creating fans, it was indisputable that Presley had become a superstar.

Elvis Presley Day

Controversy over his music and moves was not the only public recognition Presley received in the 1950s. On September 26, 1956, Presley returned home to his birthplace of Tupelo. The town declared it Elvis Presley Day and threw its honoree a big celebration, complete with a parade and fireworks. The mayor handed Presley the key to the city.

Ten years after he sang "Ole Shep" at the Mississippi-Alabama Fair and Dairy Show, Presley stepped onto the

Too Far, Too Fast

Within the span of one year, Presley went from being a total unknown to a household name. Although his rapid rise to fame was thrilling, it was also terrifying. He was afraid of burning out too soon—that fans would tire of him and move on to the next big artist. "You know, I could go out like a light, just like I came on," he said.[4]

The constant frenzy of female attention also had its ups and downs. One reporter described the screaming at Presley's shows like the roar of a jet plane. Fans stampeded him wherever he went, once trapping Presley inside an elevator. "It's getting where I can't even leave the house without something happening to me," he said.[5]

same stage. This time, 100 members of the US National Guard were brought in to control the massive crowd of excited fans.

By October of that year, Presley had sold 10 million records. He had been signed to a three-movie contract. His face was everywhere, staring out from store shelves on all kinds of merchandise, including board games, belts, stuffed hound dogs, and Love Me Tender perfume. Presley had conquered music and merchandising. Now he was headed to Hollywood, California, to take on the movie industry.

Presley Settles Down?

Even as hordes of women chased after him, it looked as though Presley might be ready to settle down with one special girl in 1956. That girl was 18-year-old June Juanico from Biloxi, Mississippi.

During an idyllic summer, Presley and Juanico vacationed together in Biloxi and fell madly in love. One night, Presley asked Juanico if she would marry him—but they had to wait three years because Presley's manager did not want a woman to get in the way of Presley's career.

As Presley's fame grew, though, Juanico found she was no longer the only woman in his life. He started seeing a movie star and a Las Vegas showgirl, among other women. Eventually there was little room left for Juanico in Presley's heart. In 1957, they broke up.

▲ Presley's ever-growing fame and adoration from other women led to a breakup with girlfriend June Juanico.

6

Presley Goes to Hollywood

With his good looks and larger-than-life persona, it was only a matter of time before Presley made his debut on the big screen. In the spring of 1956, he traveled to Hollywood for his first screen test. He had never acted before, but he wanted to be a serious actor like James Dean, a popular movie star in the 1950s.

Presley read a scene for producer Hal Wallis, and Wallis was impressed. He agreed to pay Presley $450,000 (approximately $3.7 million today) for a three-movie deal. Filming began

▸ Presley's first film was originally titled *The Reno Brothers*, but it was renamed *Love Me Tender* after a song in the film that was anticipated to be a hit.

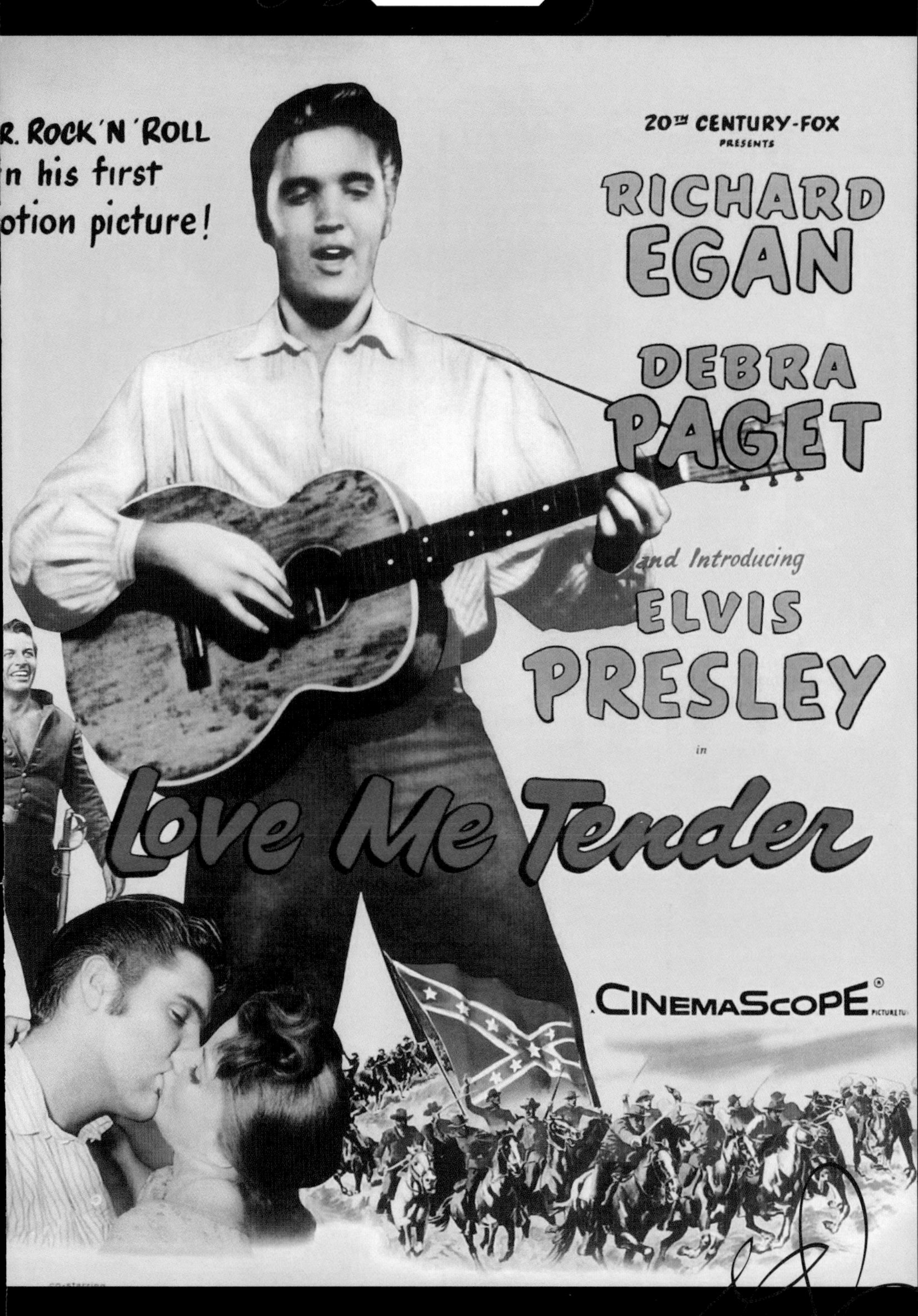
R. ROCK 'N 'ROLL
n his first
otion picture!
20TH CENTURY-FOX
PRESENTS
RICHARD
EGAN
DEBRA
PAGET
and Introducing
ELVIS
PRESLEY
in
Love Me Tender
CINEMASCOPE

that summer, amid Presley's flurry of television variety-show performances. The first film he shot was the Civil War–era Western *Love Me Tender*. The film premiered on November 15. Presley also sang several songs for the sound track—including the title song.

Far from being the serious role Presley wanted, *Love Me Tender* was little more than a lighthearted attempt to showcase the popular singer. Critics panned the film and Presley's acting. A *New York Times* critic said Presley's acting was not much more impressive than that of the horses in the movie. *Love Me Tender* made a much better impression at the box office, earning $9 million, the equivalent of nearly $75 million today.

Spurred by the commercial success of *Love Me Tender*, Wallis put Presley to work on his second film, *Loving You*, in January 1957. Presley played a talented musician who is discovered while working as a deliveryman. The story was pulled straight from Presley's own life. The movie spawned two hit singles, "Teddy Bear" and "Loving You." It also led to a new look for Presley. He dyed his hair black for the film, and he liked it so much he kept it dark for the rest of his career. His black pompadour and ducktail hairstyle became a part of his iconic image.

▲ ACCORDING TO SOME HISTORIANS, PRESLEY'S DANCE NUMBER TO THE TITLE SONG IN *JAILHOUSE ROCK* PAVED THE WAY FOR THE MODERN MUSIC VIDEO.

Presley's third movie was *Jailhouse Rock*, a story about a con man who decides to become a musician while in jail. To hone his acting technique for the role, Presley studied the work of serious actors he admired. Many critics felt *Jailhouse Rock* was Presley's best performance.

Presley Influences a Generation's Style

Conformity was common in US style in the early 1950s. Teenagers often wore the same basic uniform outfit—khaki pants or jeans and a t-shirt or button-down shirt. Then Presley came along. All of a sudden, kids were growing their hair long and emulating Presley's greased-back ducktail. They were wearing dress slacks and brightly colored shirts. Following his lead, teenagers were creating a rock-and-roll style—a flashy look to go with the electrifying new sound that was reshaping their culture.

Presley's music in the film was just as successful. The film's sound track leapt up the charts, including the title track, which became Presley's eighth Number 1 single.

Graceland

Even while Presley earned millions of dollars from his record sales, movies, and merchandise, he lived at home with his parents. In March 1957, he finally bought a place of his own—an 18-room mansion on 13.8 acres (5.3 ha) of land outside Memphis. The process was swift. Presley put down a $1,000 cash deposit on March 17, agreed to purchase the home on March 19, and the closing was set for a week later on March 26. Including the deposit, Presley paid $102,500 for the property—the approximate equivalent of $800,000 today.

The colonial-style mansion was built in 1939 and named Graceland after a relative of the previous owner. It had soaring white columns and a huge gate out front, which Presley adorned with giant metal guitarists and musical notes. Inside the front hallway the blue ceiling was designed to look like a night sky, complete with flickering stars. Presley made several upgrades to the house, adding a swimming pool and eight-foot (2.4 m) stone fence outside and a working soda fountain inside. He later added a trophy room to hold his growing collection of gold and platinum records.

Presley moved into Graceland in June 1957. His parents soon joined him. Presley designed a special garden for his mother, where she could look over a menagerie of chickens, geese, ducks, turkeys, and hens. Graceland was also home to dogs, monkeys, peacocks, hogs, and donkeys—it was like the Presleys' own mini zoo.

Presley surrounded himself with family and friends at Graceland. They

Gathering at the Graceland Gates

There was almost always a crowd outside Graceland. Eager fans would gather outside the wide front gates at all hours of the day and night, hoping for a glimpse of their idol. They were often lucky. Presley was known to drive in one of his cars or ride on horseback to the gates to grace fans with an impromptu autograph session.

When Presley was away, the guards sometimes let fans through the gates onto the grounds to take pictures in front of the mansion. When Presley was home, certain fans were sometimes allowed to enter not only the grounds, but his home as well—the prettiest female fans occasionally got a personal invitation to hang out with him and his entourage inside Graceland. The constant stream of fans flocking to Graceland continues long after Presley's death.

would all sit on his custom 15-foot (5 m) white sofa inside his den and watch television. They would play pool and listen to records on the jukebox, but never his own music—Presley did not like listening to himself when he was not recording or performing. It was a tight-knit family. But the group would soon be broken up when Presley was sent overseas to serve his country.

Gladys's Drinking

Despite Graceland's lush surroundings and the garden created especially for her, Gladys never quite felt at home there. She felt lonely, eclipsed by her son's new fame and fortune. She worried about him constantly. In her fear and loneliness, Gladys often turned to drinking for comfort.

▲ PRESLEY AT GRACELAND IN 1957

7

Presley in the Army

Just before Christmas 1957, Presley received an unexpected draft notice informing him he would have to serve in the US Army. Before the military became all-volunteer in 1973, many young men were drafted to serve, and celebrities were no exception. Presley was granted a 60-day deferment to finish his fourth movie, *King Creole*. He was inducted into the army on March 24, 1958. He shipped out to Fort Hood, Texas, for basic training a few days later.

▸ Presley received a crew cut as part of being processed into the army.

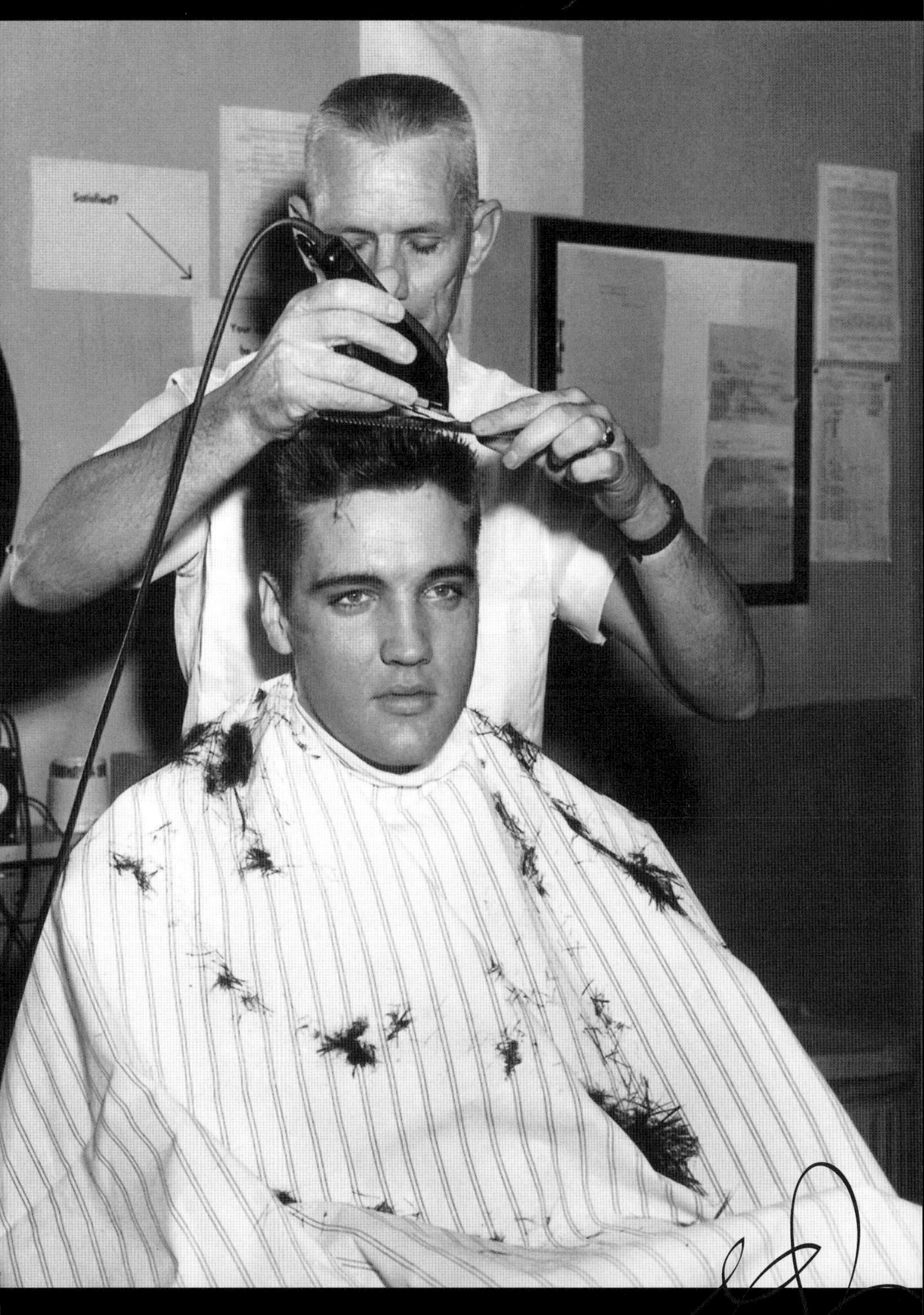

Presley trained with the Second Armored Division in Texas for six months. When he first arrived, the other recruits in his division gave him a hard time. But when they saw how hard he worked in basic training, they began treating him just like one of the troops.

"Everything I Have Is Gone"

Presley moved his parents into a three-bedroom trailer home near Fort Hood so they could be close to him. While Presley trained over the summer, his mother's health declined. On August 8, she was rushed back to Memphis to be hospitalized for treatment. Years of heavy drinking had taken their

The Most Famous Haircut in History

Long hair did not cut it in the US military. So, before heading to basic training, Presley needed to rid himself of his thick, dark hair. This upset fans to no end. Three teenage girls from Montana appealed to President Eisenhower himself, begging him to at least spare Presley's sideburns.

On March 25, 1958, the day after he was officially sworn in, Presley took a bus to Fort Chaffee, Arkansas, to be processed into the military before heading to Fort Hood for basic training. In Fort Chaffee, he received what may have been the most famous haircut in history. Parker arranged for more than 50 reporters and photographers to be at the barbershop to capture the moment. He wanted everyone in America to know what a good, patriotic boy Presley was. As his hair fell to the floor, Presley joked, "Hair today, gone tomorrow."[1] The snappy saying would continue to live on long after Presley's death. Today, visitors to Fort Chaffee can see video and photos of the famous haircut at the Chaffee Barbershop Museum.

toll on her liver, which had become scarred and damaged.

Presley was granted an emergency leave from the army to be by his mother's side. On August 14, 1958, Gladys passed away at the age of 46. Presley was overwhelmed with grief. At her funeral, Presley threw himself onto his mother's coffin, wailing, "Oh, God! Everything I have is gone."[2] Gladys was buried at Forest Hill Cemetery, just a few miles down the road from Graceland.

After his mother's death, Presley wanted to give up. Nothing seemed important anymore. But he knew he had to press on and finish his military service. So on August 24, he returned to Fort Hood to complete training. Within a few weeks, Presley was shipped off to Europe.

Presley in Germany

On October 1, Presley arrived in Friedberg, a town in southern Germany, to serve as a member of the First Medium Tank Battalion, Thirty-Second Armor. More than 1,000 eager fans were waiting there to welcome him.

While stationed in Germany, Presley lived off base in a three-story, five-bedroom home in the nearby town of Bad Nauheim. Presley brought his father and grandmother to stay in the house with

▲ Presley, shown in Germany, achieved Private First Class rank during his stint with the army.

him, along with a couple of Memphis friends to act as his security guards.

When Presley was not actively serving his country, he and his friends were making mischief in Germany and neighboring France. They pulled a number of stunts, such as wrecking cars and setting off fireworks in their hotel rooms. Presley also got friendly with some of the local girls and would soon meet the woman who would become his wife.

Meeting Cilla

In August 1959, 14-year-old Priscilla Beaulieu had just moved from Texas to Germany with her stepfather, who was an army captain. Her biological father, a navy pilot, had died in a plane crash when Priscilla was just six months old.

Presley Gets His Black Belt

Presley spent much of his free time in Germany studying karate. Under the tutelage of a local martial arts teacher, he earned his first-degree black belt. Presley continued studying karate for most of his life. In the mid-1970s, he became an eighth-degree black belt—the third highest rank.

Priscilla's life in Germany revolved around school until September 13, 1959 when she attended a party at Presley's home. Priscilla arrived at the party and Presley, who was 24 at the time, was smitten with her right away. He played the piano and sang "Are You Lonesome Tonight?," locking eyes with her the whole time.

After the party, Presley asked Priscilla if he could see her again. She asked her parents for permission. They did not approve at first because of Presley's ten-year age difference, but Presley soon won them over. He promised them his intentions toward their daughter were honorable.

For some reason, Presley felt more comfortable with Priscilla than he had with any other girl. He felt as though only she understood his loneliness.

▲ PRISCILLA BEAULIEU HOLDS A PHOTOGRAPH OF PRESLEY ON MARCH 1, 1960, THE DAY BEFORE HE IS SCHEDULED TO LEAVE GERMANY.

As he had with his mother, Presley gave Priscilla a special nickname—"Cilla."

GOING HOME

Being in love with Priscilla did not stop Presley from leaving Germany once his military service ended. After promising Cilla he would send for her soon, Presley left Germany on March 2, 1960, to return home to restart his music career.

Upon his homecoming, Presley was more popular than ever. Two weeks after returning from Germany, he recorded a comeback album titled *Elvis Is Back!* The singles "Stuck on You," "Are You Lonesome Tonight?," and "It's Now or Never" all rose to Number 1.

While he was away, Presley's image had transformed. Gone was the rebel. In his place was a more mainstream pop singer, which played up the patriotic image he gained by serving in the military. This new image was broadcast in March 1960, when Presley taped the *Welcome Home Elvis* special. Presley wore a suit and tie on the show and barely shook or wiggled as he sang, but the girls still screamed and his fans still loved him.

A Dangerous Habit

Americans saw an image of a patriotic, wholesome Presley going off to serve his country. But behind the scenes, Presley was becoming darker and moodier. He felt lonely and isolated by his fame. It was during his time in Germany that he started taking prescription drugs. A doctor prescribed amphetamines (also called speed) because at the time the dangerous drugs were believed to provide energy and help control a person's weight. "They will give you more strength and energy than you can imagine," Presley boasted to a friend.[3] They were also highly addictive and had negative side effects such as restlessness, irritability, insomnia, and depression. Presley thought of the drugs as harmless because a doctor had prescribed them. He did not realize how much destruction they would eventually cause in his life.

8

Money, Movies, and Love

Presley's recording career was booming upon his return home from his time in the military. He was earning $1 million a movie. But under the surface, trouble was brewing.

Although Presley was busy making music and movies after his return home, he was not doing his best work. He acted in an average of three films a year in the early 1960s—but they were formula pictures such as *G.I. Blues*, *Girls! Girls! Girls!*, and *Blue Hawaii*. Each film was almost exactly the same: set in some exotic location,

▸ *GIRLS! GIRLS! GIRLS!* SHOWCASES THEMES THAT ARE COMMON IN ALL PRESLEY'S MOVIES.

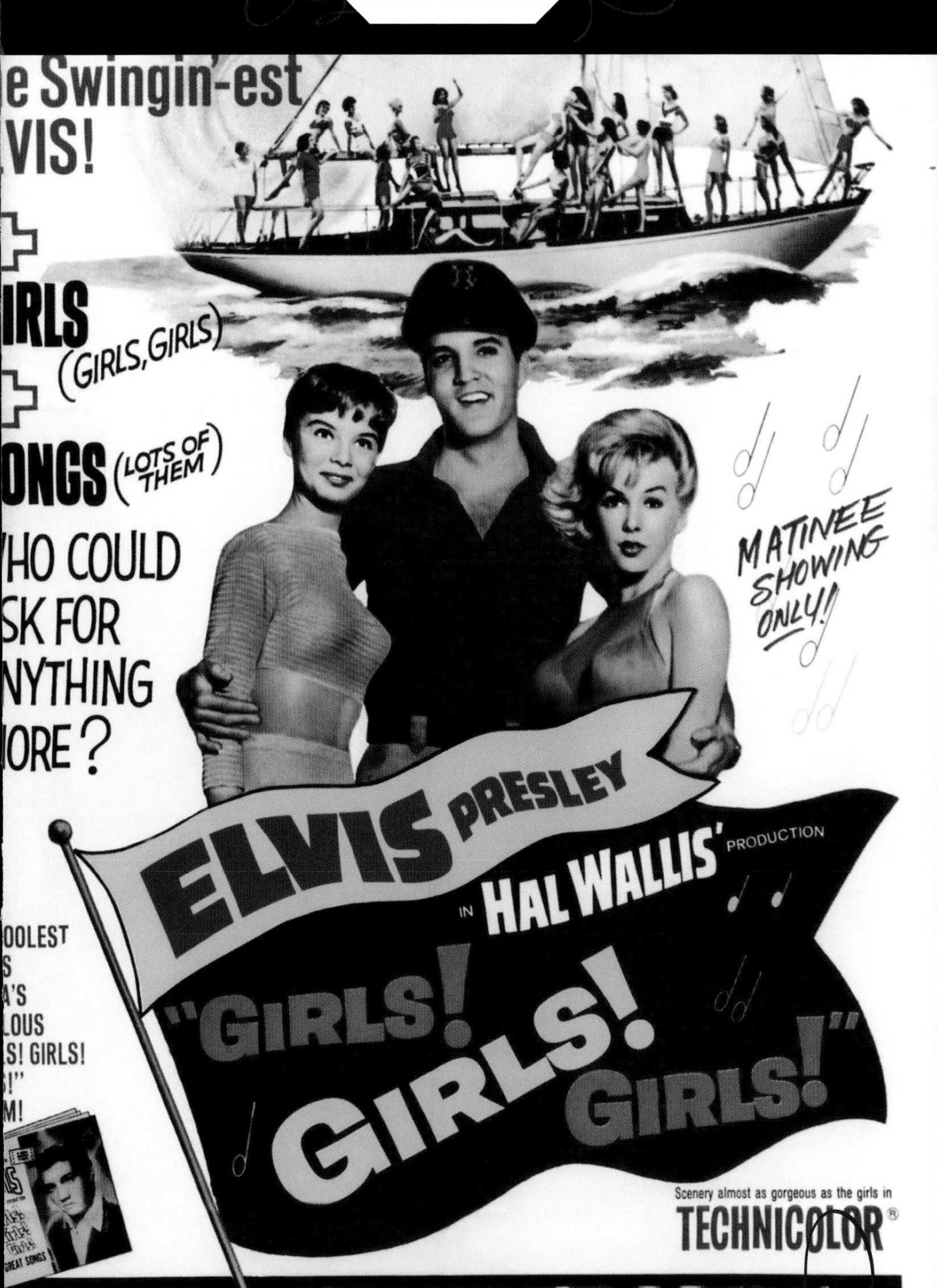
e Swingin'-est
VIS!
IRLS
(GIRLS, GIRLS)
ONGS
(LOTS OF THEM)
HO COULD
SK FOR
NYTHING
ORE?
MATINEE SHOWING ONLY!
ELVIS PRESLEY
IN HAL WALLIS' PRODUCTION
"GIRLS! GIRLS! GIRLS!"
Scenery almost as gorgeous as the girls in
TECHNICOLOR®

with Presley surrounded by beautiful women in bikinis. He would get into a few fights to prove his toughness, sing some songs, and fall in love.

Presley grew tired of the imitation films, but whenever he asked to act in more serious roles, Parker, who controlled Presley's music and movie career, said no. The money from Presley's movies—and their sound tracks—was just too good.

Spending Spree

The money from his movies was pouring into Presley's bank account. Yet he was spending it almost as quickly as he earned it.

Presley was extremely generous to friends and family. He would fly himself and members of his entourage—called the Memphis Mafia—to Las Vegas, Nevada, on a whim. In Memphis, he would rent out the fairgrounds, roller rink, or local movie theater to entertain his friends. He would give family and friends jewelry, cars, and even houses. Sometimes he would give gifts to total strangers just to see their reactions. "I love the idea of overwhelming a total

The Memphis Mafia

As his fame grew, Presley surrounded himself with friends and family members who protected and took care of him. They became known as the Memphis Mafia because of the black suits they wore. The Memphis Mafia included, among others, Presley's cousins Billy and Gene Smith and his father, Vernon.

▲ The pink Cadillac Presley bought Gladys is on display at Graceland. Presley loved gifting Cadillacs, once buying 14 for his band members.

stranger with a gift of a new car, just because they happened to be nearby," he said. "It's an incredible kick."[1] Presley also bought himself several cars—his favorites were Cadillacs—as well as motorcycles and go-karts to speed around Graceland. Later, he even bought his own fleet of airplanes. Vernon was in charge of the finances, but he could do little to reign in his son's lavish spending.

Spending too much money was only part of Presley's troubling behavior. He was also regularly using drugs. He started taking amphetamines in Germany and then began using a drug cocktail of stimulants, sleeping pills, and painkillers. The stimulants helped him stay awake each day, and the sleeping pills helped him sleep at night. Possibly because of the drugs, his moods shifted quickly—and radically. When Presley was in one of his foul moods, everyone at Graceland knew to tiptoe around him.

Priscilla Comes to Graceland

While Presley focused on his career and life at Graceland, Priscilla was attending high school in Germany. She dreamed of the day when she might finally become Mrs. Elvis Presley. Presley would call her from time to time, but back in the states he dated other women, including a former girlfriend, actress Anita Wood, who was staying at Graceland in early 1962.

In March 1962, Presley flew Priscilla from Germany to visit him in Los Angeles, California, where he had just finished filming the movie *Girls! Girls! Girls!* By the end of the summer, Wood had moved out of Graceland and announced to the press she and Presley had broken up.

After her visit to Los Angeles, Presley persuaded Priscilla's parents to let her move to Memphis to finish high school. He promised them his plan was to marry her one day. Priscilla moved to Memphis and into Graceland in March 1963. She enrolled at Immaculate Conception High School, an all-girls high school.

While Priscilla lived at Graceland, the media had no idea she existed. Presley kept her a secret because she was still underage. If the press found out he was dating a teenager, it would have been scandalous. Presley left Priscilla alone and secreted away at Graceland for long stretches of time while he filmed movies—and dated other women—in Los Angeles.

Larry Geller and a More Spiritual Presley

Presley was an avid reader and always wanted to learn something new. He especially loved to read about Eastern philosophy and spirituality. Although he was raised as a Christian, he always searched for greater meaning in his life.

On his road to self-discovery, Presley met Larry Geller in 1964. Geller was a Beverly Hills hairdresser who eventually became Presley's hair stylist, but he was also interested in meditation, yoga, and Eastern spiritual practices. He and Presley began having long, serious talks about religion and philosophy.

Presley's friends thought Geller was a fraud who was trying to push Presley into some kind of cult. Finally, Parker had enough. In 1967, he kicked Geller out of Presley's inner circle. He said the books Geller encouraged Presley to read cluttered his mind, leaving him less time to make music—and money.

Presley and Priscilla Tie the Knot

Although Presley had been dating other women, in 1966, it appeared he was finally ready to settle down with 21-year-old Priscilla and fulfill the promise he made to her parents. For Christmas that year he gave Priscilla two presents. One was a black quarter horse, which she named Domino. The other was a three-and-a-half carat diamond engagement ring.

Presley then found a new home to share with his bride-to-be. It was a farmhouse on 160 acres (65 ha) of rolling green hills in Horn Lake, Mississippi.

Presley paid $437,000, approximately $3 million today, for the farm, which he named Circle G Ranch—the "G" stood for Graceland. He filled it with horses and cattle and invited his circle of friends and family to join him there. He bought them all trailers so everyone could live together like cowboys on the ranch. Presley and Priscilla shared a three-bedroom trailer surrounded by a white picket fence. They had barbecues and target shoots, and they went horseback riding. Within just a few weeks, Presley had spent nearly $1 million on his new property.

On May 1, 1967, just months after proposing and setting up their newest home, Presley and

▲ PRESLEY AND PRISCILLA WITH NEWBORN DAUGHTER LISA MARIE

Priscilla were married at the Aladdin Hotel in Las Vegas. Only 14 of their family members and closest friends attended the ceremony. A bigger reception was held at Graceland three weeks later.

That summer, Priscilla announced she was pregnant. On February 1, 1968, daughter Lisa Marie Presley was born at Baptist Hospital in Memphis. When news spread that Presley was a father, fans flooded the hospital with flowers, cards, gifts, and hundreds of phone calls asking about little Lisa Marie.

The Beatles Meet Their Idol

1964 was the year of the Beatles. The British band of four had broken onto the US music scene in a huge way. They were wildly popular with fans and successful in the music industry. During the week of April 4, they held the top five spots in the *Billboard* Singles chart.

While in Los Angeles in August of that year, the Beatles wanted more than anything to meet Presley. He was their idol. "We all wanted to be Elvis," Beatles member John Lennon said.[2] On August 27, the Beatles arrived at the Bel Air home where Presley stayed when he was filming movies.

At first, the Beatles were so in awe of Presley they did not say a word. Finally, Presley spoke up. "If you guys are just gonna sit there and stare at me, I'm going to bed," he said.[3] That broke the ice. They all had a laugh. Presley picked up a guitar and started playing. Beatles members Lennon and Paul McCartney strummed along. They played a few songs—some by Presley, some by the Beatles, and some by other artists. Lennon later said the meeting "was the greatest night of my life."[4]

The Comeback Special

The year 1968 was a time of great change not only for new father Presley but also for the world, which was facing events such as the Vietnam War and the assassination of civil rights leader Martin Luther King Jr. Music was undergoing big changes, too. Singer-songwriters such as Bob Dylan and Jim Morrison of the Doors were rising in popularity. British pop group the Beatles stormed the world with a contemporary sound and mod style. Presley's music seemed old fashioned by comparison—almost obsolete. With a string of bad movies and copycat sound tracks, his career was in a slump.

Then NBC called wanting Presley to do a television special. For the first time in seven years, he would be performing in front of a live audience. The show's producer, Steve Binder, was fascinated by Presley and wanted to bring back the old Elvis—the rebellious, exciting Elvis.

During the show, called simply *Elvis* and later dubbed *The Comeback Special*, Presley wore a black leather suit. He performed his biggest hits. At the end of the show, Presley appeared alone on stage in a white suit, standing in front of a backdrop of lights that spelled his name. He sang, "If I Can Dream," a powerful song about the assassinations of Martin Luther King Jr. and Senator Robert Kennedy. It became one of his most famous performances.

The special aired on December 3, 1968. Nearly half of US households watching television tuned in. A new generation of fans was introduced to Presley's music. In 1996, *TV Guide* named the special Number 63 in its 100 Most Memorable Moments in TV History.

▲ PRESLEY ONSTAGE DURING *THE COMEBACK SPECIAL*

The Comeback Special breathed new life into Presley's career. He promised never to get sucked into the same old movie/sound track routine again. "I will never sing a song I don't believe in again. I will never make another movie I don't believe in again," he vowed.[5] Shortly after the special, Presley went into a Memphis studio and recorded an album of original songs. They were some of the best songs of his career, including "Suspicious Minds," "I Can't Stop Loving You," and "In the Ghetto." He was back to his gospel, soul, country, and blues roots. The album was a huge success, which meant it was time for Presley to focus on live performances again.

Presley's Gospel Album

After putting out a string of predictable movie sound tracks, Presley wanted to try something different. In 1966, he recorded his first gospel album, *How Great Thou Art,* at RCA studios in Nashville. Presley handpicked songs such as "In the Garden," "By and By," and "Farther Along" and worked on the arrangements himself. He wanted the album to be absolutely perfect. When *How Great Thou Art* was released in 1967, it earned Presley three Grammy Awards.

9

Viva Las Vegas

Presley was back at the top of his game. Where better to showcase his new music and live performances than in a city that was booming with life? After World War II, the city of Las Vegas became a mecca for casinos and live entertainment. By 1967, 14 million visitors a year were traveling there to eat, gamble, and be entertained.

The International Hotel, later renamed the Las Vegas Hilton, was the biggest hotel in Las Vegas. It had a showroom that held an audience

▸ The flashy white jumpsuit Presley wore during his Las Vegas years became forever connected with his image.

of more than 1,700 people. On July 31, 1969, Presley opened there to a sold-out crowd.

Presley's first long Las Vegas engagement lasted four weeks and included 57 shows. In those early performances, he wore an all-black suit. In later years, his wardrobe changed to a white rhinestone-studded jumpsuit with a superman cape and a huge belt buckle. It is the outfit most often associated with Presley and the one his impersonators still wear today.

In his Las Vegas show, Presley performed a medley of his old classics and new hits, as well as covers of songs from other artists. Fans came from all over the world to see him. In one month, he pulled in $1.5 million in ticket sales. Parker signed a five-year, $1 million contract

Outstanding Young American

On January 16, 1971, the Junior Chambers of Commerce (Jaycees) presented Presley with an award for being one of the Top Ten Outstanding Young Americans.

During his speech, Presley said, "When I was a child, ladies and gentlemen, I was a dreamer. I read comic books, and I was the hero of the comic book. I saw movies, and I was the hero in the movie. So every dream I ever dreamed has come true a hundred times."[1] Presley was so proud of his award he carried it around with him everywhere he went for many years.

Also that year, Presley received the Bing Crosby Award from the National Academy of Recording Arts and Sciences (later named the Lifetime Achievement Award). He was just 36 years old.

to make Presley a Las Vegas regular.

During the weeks Presley was not in Las Vegas, he was busy touring. Presley did so many shows while on tour that after each performance, he would run from the stage into a waiting car and be whisked straight to the airport. To quiet the hysterical crowd, the announcer used the phrase coined during Presley's earlier performing years, "Elvis has left the building."[2] The phrase became forever linked with Presley.

Fame and Fear

Presley's fame had its pros and cons. One of the biggest drawbacks was the risk that someone might try to hurt him. In the summer of 1970, someone slid a note under Presley's Las Vegas hotel-room door that read, "I am going to kill you."[3] Presley was on edge during that night's show. He performed with a small pistol tucked inside his boot, just in case anyone tried to attack him. Although he finished the concert without a problem, Presley's paranoia continued. He never felt totally safe again. To protect himself, he spent thousands of dollars amassing a huge gun collection.

Presley and Priscilla Split

Presley's rigorous touring schedule was hard on Priscilla. She stayed busy taking care of Lisa Marie and redecorating the new home they bought in Los Angeles, but it was not enough. She was also tired of Presley's wild spending habits and reading in magazines about all the other women he was seeing. In February 1972, Priscilla flew out to see Presley in Las Vegas. Reluctantly, she told him she

▲ PRISCILLA AND PRESLEY APPEARED IN COURT FOR THEIR DIVORCE HEARING. THEY REMAINED CLOSE FRIENDS AFTER THEY SPLIT.

was leaving him. “It broke my heart,” she recalled. “I had to save my daughter and myself. I had to make a life of my own.”[4]

Presley was hurt and angry, but he still had a full schedule of concerts to keep up. In June 1972, he played four shows to sold-out crowds at New York’s Madison Square Garden. The concerts were taped for the documentary *Elvis on Tour*, which earned a Golden Globe Award in 1973.

Presley and Priscilla’s divorce was finalized on October 9, 1973. As busy as Presley was, he still made time to see Lisa Marie after the split. He also found time to meet women. One of those women was 22-year-old Linda Thompson. For the next four years, she would be the main relationship in his life—his confidant, love, and, eventually, his nurse.

Aloha From Hawaii

Presley did many shows in Las Vegas between 1970 and 1973, but one of his most famous performances during that time took place in Hawaii. The *Elvis: Aloha from Hawaii* television special aired from Honolulu on January 14, 1973. Audiences from around the world—including Australia, South Korea, Japan, and the Philippines—watched the show. The sound track to the special stayed on the pop charts for a full year.

To the whole world, it seemed as though Presley was at the pinnacle of his career. But behind closed doors, he was falling apart.

Drugs and Paranoia

Presley kept up a grueling touring schedule in the 1970s. He performed more than 1,000 concerts between 1969 and 1977, not including his regular Las Vegas shows. He was exhausted.

Presley put several doctors on his payroll to supply him with drugs to keep him going. In addition to the amphetamines and sleeping pills he was already taking, he added a variety of drugs to treat the back pain and other ailments that plagued him. Because he had prescriptions for the drugs, Presley stubbornly refused to believe he was an addict.

Angry at the Colonel

Though he trusted Parker early in his career, by 1973 Presley had grown fed up with his manager controlling his every move. Backstage at the Las Vegas Hilton one night after a show, Presley blew up at Parker. Parker responded by calling Presley ungrateful. Enraged, Presley fired Parker. After a week or two, though, Presley realized how much he needed his longtime manager and rehired him.

During 1973, Presley accidentally overdosed several times. One night, a doctor had to revive him at his Las Vegas hotel suite—he nearly died. In October, he was rushed to Baptist Hospital in Memphis. Not only had he overdosed again but he had a fatty liver that was failing, as well as ulcers and glaucoma. The press was told Presley was just exhausted. However, family and friends knew the truth. Although they may have been concerned for him, Presley continued on his destructive path. Girlfriend Thompson cared for him round the clock.

In addition to the drugs and health problems, Presley developed a paranoid fear that somebody was going to kill him. He had violent temper outbursts and carried guns with him at all times.

Once, he talked about wanting to hire a hit man to kill Priscilla's karate-instructor boyfriend.

Life on Lonely Street

Though he felt miserable from exhaustion and drug use, Presley had to keep up his touring schedule to pay all the people—from musicians to bodyguards—who depended on him. When he was in Las Vegas, he did two shows a day, seven days a week.

Presley's only comforts were drugs and food. He lived on a steady diet of cheeseburgers, bacon, and cake, not to mention his favorite food, fried peanut butter and banana sandwiches. As his weight ballooned, reporters wrote snide comments about Presley's weight. When he turned 40 in 1975, the *National Enquirer* ran a story titled, "Elvis at 40—Paunchy, Depressed & Living in Fear."[5] It hurt Presley to be ridiculed this way.

It is unclear whether the media was aware of Presley's drug use while he was alive, but there were likely suspicions. Reporters noted that Presley would sometimes act odd during concerts. The drugs Presley took made him do strange things onstage. Sometimes he rambled incoherently. Often he forgot the lyrics to his own songs. Once he apologized to fans before passing out right in the middle of a performance. It became common for audience members to walk out during his shows. Presley had become a joke.

Final Performances

By 1975, Presley was run down and worn out. His doctor asked Parker to cut back on his heavy touring schedule. Parker refused.

Presley felt so awful by 1976 that he could not even make it into the studio to record his next album. He had the equipment brought to Graceland and recorded an album of songs at home while exhausted and in constant pain. At the time he wrote, "I don't know who I can talk to anymore . . . I feel lost sometimes."[6]

Thompson became overwhelmed by Presley's medical and emotional needs. In November 1976, she left him. He soon found another love, 20-year-old beauty queen Ginger Alden, who was 21 years younger than him. Just before Christmas, Presley proposed to Alden, presenting her with a large diamond engagement ring. She said yes.

The number of Presley's shows dwindled in late 1976 and early 1977. When he performed at the Philadelphia Spectrum on May 28, 1977, he was so unhealthy he was panting between songs. He forgot his own lyrics and staggered around

▲ PRESLEY IN JUNE 1977, DURING ONE OF HIS LAST PERFORMANCES

the stage. Yet washed-up or not, Presley was still a legend, and he kept getting booked for shows.

In June, Presley performed in Indianapolis, Indiana. CBS recorded the concert for an upcoming special. Though he looked bloated, shaky, and confused, his voice was still strong. It was Presley's final performance.

10

THE KING IS GONE

Worn down and weary, Presley returned home to Graceland. In the early morning hours of August 16, 1977, he was having trouble sleeping. After playing a game of racquetball at the court behind his home to pass the time, he went up to his bedroom, but he still could not fall asleep. To avoid disturbing his fiancée, Alden, Presley went into the bathroom to read.

That was where Alden, who had gone to bed in the early morning hours and slept late, found

▸ THE DEATH OF THE KING OF ROCK AND ROLL MADE HEADLINES AROUND THE WORLD.

DAILY NEWS

Cloudy and humid, showers. Low 80s. Sunny tomorrow. Details page 87

New York, Wednesday, August 17, 1977

Price: 20 cents

ELVIS PRESLEY DIES AT 42

Singer Suffers Heart Attack

Berkowitz Pleads Innocent; Plans Insanity Defense

Stories on pages 3, 12 and 33

Report Carter Picks Ala. Judge As FBI Chief

him at 2:30 the following afternoon—lying facedown on the bathroom floor. He was not moving, and he did not appear to be breathing. Alden called for Presley's bodyguards.

Presley was rushed to nearby Baptist Memorial Hospital. Doctors frantically tried to revive him. On August 16, 1977, at approximately 3:30 p.m., Presley was pronounced dead. He was just 42 years old.

The official cause of death was heart failure, but for years afterward, experts would argue over what really killed Presley. Was it his appetite for unhealthy food? Was it his weak heart? Or was it the massive cocktail of drugs that was found in his system?

"Elvis Presley's death deprives our country of a part of itself. He was unique, irreplaceable. More than twenty years ago, he burst upon the scene with an impact that was unprecedented and will probably never be equaled. His music and his personality, fusing the styles of white country and black rhythm and blues, permanently changed the face of American popular culture. His following was immense. And he was a symbol to people the world over of the vitality, rebelliousness and good humor of this country."[1]

—President Jimmy Carter in 1977

Word of Presley's death spread quickly. Almost every television newscast led with the story. Newspapers screamed the news with bold headlines. Flags across the South were lowered to half-staff—a sign of respect and mourning. Memphis

▲ Thousands of fans flooded Graceland to mourn Presley on August 17, 1977.

radio stations observed two minutes of silence in Presley's honor.

By the afternoon of August 17, tens of thousands of fans had lined up outside Graceland, with more streaming in throughout the day. The Graceland gates were opened so fans could walk in single file past Presley's casket inside the mansion to say their final goodbyes. Many fans sobbed. A few collapsed at the sight of their idol lying dead in his coffin.

Presley was buried on August 18. A white Cadillac hearse carrying Presley's casket led the funeral procession, followed by 16 white limousines. As they drove from Graceland down a part of Highway 51 that had been renamed Elvis Presley Boulevard a few years earlier, thousands of people lined the streets to watch the procession pass. Presley was laid to rest at Forest Hill Cemetery in a mausoleum near his mother's grave.

THE KING LIVES

Presley's death did not kill his career. If anything, it provoked a renewed interest in his music and movies. In the weeks following his death, radio stations began playing Presley's songs again, and his records once again started flying off store shelves.

Presley also received several awards after his death. In 1986, Presley was one of the first musicians

Parker Makes One Last Deal

The dirt had barely settled over Presley's casket when Parker started angling to extend his management deal. He realized he could make even more money with Presley gone, and he wanted to make sure he profited from the singer's posthumous career. Still grieving over the loss of his son, Vernon signed a new contract giving Parker rights to Presley's work forever. The new contract allowed Parker to make more money from the Presley name than Presley's own family.

In 1980, Priscilla and other family members took Parker to court, challenging him for the right to Presley's name and earnings. The judge in the case sided with the Presleys, charging Parker with "enriching himself by mismanaging Presley's career."[2] All royalties from the sales of records, films, and merchandise dating back to 1973 would go straight to his estate.

to be inducted into the Rock and Roll Hall of Fame. In 1987, the American Music Awards posthumously gave him its Award of Merit. He was also inducted into the Country Music and Gospel Halls of Fame after his death.

Gladys and Elvis Return to Graceland

Presley was first buried at Forest Hill Cemetery near his mother. But when several people tried to vandalize his grave, he was moved to the Graceland Meditation Garden. His mother was moved there, too. Vernon joined his wife and son there when he died in 1979.

Priscilla decided to preserve the home where she and Presley had lived, turning Graceland into a memorial where fans could go to remember their idol. On June 7, 1982, Graceland opened its doors to the public. Every year, 500,000 people visit to get a glimpse of Presley's gold and platinum albums, pink Cadillac, and US Army uniform. Every August 15 into the early hours of August 16, the anniversary of his death, thousands gather for a candlelight vigil. Today, Graceland is on the national register of historic places, and it is the second most-visited home in the country, just after the White House.

Since his death, Presley's image and memory have been everywhere. He has a club on Beale Street in Memphis (they serve his favorite food—fried peanut butter and banana sandwiches). There is a Heartbreak Hotel across the street from Graceland. And there are thousands of Elvis impersonators around the world—some of whom skydive and perform wedding ceremonies. His combined album sales, royalties, and attractions made Presley the most profitable dead musician until 2005, when grunge rocker Kurt Cobain knocked him out of the top spot.

PRESLEY'S LEGACY

A plaque outside Presley's childhood home in Tupelo states, "Presley's career as a singer and entertainer redefined popular music."[3] Presley challenged the idea of what music should sound like. He blurred the distinction between African-American and white music, sold more than a billion records in his lifetime and beyond, and broke records that still stand today—including the most Top Forty hits with 104 hits, most Top Ten hits with 38 hits, and most weeks at Number 1 with 80 weeks.

Is Presley Still Alive?

He was an extra in a scene of the 1990 movie *Home Alone*. He was spotted shopping for hair-styling gel at a Richmond, Virginia, Walmart. He saved a woman from drowning in Saint Petersburg, Florida. He even made a secret phone call to former president Bill Clinton. There are many eyewitnesses who claim Presley is still alive—people who believe they've spotted him just about everywhere. The 1988 book *Is Elvis Alive?* by Gail Brewer-Giorgio fueled the speculation that Presley faked his own death to escape from his fame. Is Presley still alive? The rumors and sightings continue, more than 30 years after he was buried.

▲ Presley lives on in the hearts of generations of fans.

People claim to still see Presley today, and some do not believe he is really dead. It may be because they're so reluctant to let him go. As one fan put it, "There's never been anybody like him. I don't think he'll ever die."[4]

Timeline

1935	1945	1946
Elvis Aaron Presley is born on January 8 in Tupelo, Mississippi.	On October 3, ten-year-old Presley sings at the Mississippi-Alabama Fair and Dairy Show.	On January 8, Presley gets his first guitar for his eleventh birthday.

1954	1954	1955
Presley and his band perform their first big concert, held on July 30 at the Overton Park band shell in Memphis.	Presley performs at the Grand Ole Opry on October 2.	Presley signs a contract with RCA Records on November 21.

1948	1954	1954
The Presleys move to Memphis, Tennessee, on November 6.	Presley records "That's All Right (Mama)" on July 5 with guitarist Scotty Moore and bass player Bill Black.	"That's All Right (Mama)" is released as a single on July 19.

1956	1956	1956
On January 10, Presley records "Heartbreak Hotel" for RCA.	Presley makes his television debut on January 28 on *Stage Show*.	"Heartbreak Hotel" earns Presley his first gold record on April 14.

Timeline

1956

Presley makes a historic appearance on September 9 on *The Ed Sullivan Show*.

1956

Presley's first movie, *Love Me Tender*, premieres on November 15.

1956

The "Million Dollar Quartet" partakes in a jam session on December 4 at Sun Studio.

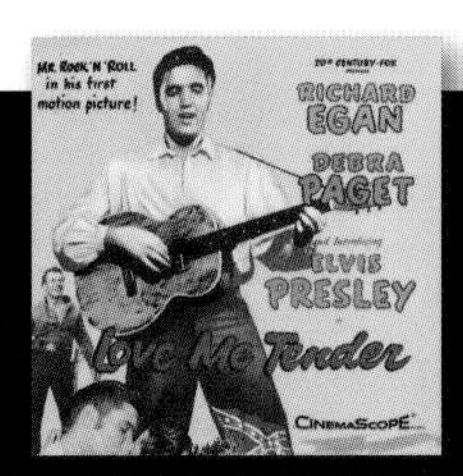

1967

Presley marries Priscilla on May 1 at the Aladdin Hotel in Las Vegas, Nevada.

1968

Priscilla gives birth to Lisa Marie Presley on February 1.

1968

Presley performs on *The Comeback Special*, which airs on December 3.

1957

Presley closes on his Graceland mansion in Memphis on March 26.

1958

Presley is inducted into the US Army on March 24.

1959

Presley meets Priscilla Beaulieu on September 13, while stationed in Germany.

1969

Presley opens a four-week show on July 31 at the International Hotel in Las Vegas.

1973

Presley and Priscilla divorce on October 9.

1977

Presley dies at Graceland on August 16.

DATE OF BIRTH
January 8, 1935

PLACE OF BIRTH
Tupelo, Mississippi

DATE OF DEATH
August 16, 1977

PLACE OF DEATH
Graceland, Memphis, Tennessee

PARENTS
Gladys and Vernon Presley

MARRIAGE
Priscilla Beaulieu (1967–1973)

CHILDREN
Lisa Marie Presley

CAREER HIGHLIGHTS

Selected Albums

Elvis Presley (1956)
Elvis (1956)
Loving You (1957)
Elvis Is Back! (1960)
G.I. Blues (1960)
His Hand in Mine (1960)
Blue Hawaii (1961)
Girls! Girls! Girls! (1962)
Elvis for Everyone! (1965)
Elvis TV Special (1969)
From Elvis in Memphis (1969)
Worldwide 50 Gold Award Hits, Vol. 1 (1970)
Elvis Country (1971)
Aloha from Hawaii via Satellite (1973)
The Sun Sessions (1976)
Elvis in Concert (1977)

Selected Films

Love Me Tender (1956)
Jailhouse Rock (1957)
GI Blues (1960)
Blue Hawaii (1961)
Girls! Girls! Girls! (1962)
It Happened at the World's Fair (1963)
Viva Las Vegas (1964)
Clambake (1967)
The Trouble with Girls (1969)

QUOTE

"The people were looking for something different and I came along just in time. I was lucky."—*Elvis Presley*

GLOSSARY

ducktail

A type of men's hairstyle that was popular in the 1950s. The hair is worn slicked back on both sides and forms a ridge in the back of the head.

emcee

The master of ceremonies at a show or performance.

entourage

A group of people who surround and travel with a celebrity or other important person.

forgery

A crime in which someone alters a document deceitfully.

impromptu

A performance that is done without being planned or rehearsed.

incoherent

Speaking in a way that is unclear and difficult for other people to understand.

mecca

A place that attracts people with a particular interest or within a particular group.

paranoia

A condition in which a person fears that others are out to get him or her—with no real cause for the fear.

pompadour
A hairstyle in which the hair is styled high above the forehead.

posthumous
Something that happens or continues after a person dies.

producer
Someone who oversees or provides money for a play, television show, movie, or album.

repossessed
A home or other property that is taken back by a lender, such as a bank, when the owner is not able to make payments on it.

royalties
Money given to an artist based on a percentage of sales.

scandalous
Something that causes public anger because it is seen as wrong or immoral.

segregated
The practice of separating by race or other category.

sharecropper
A farmer who works someone else's land in exchange for a percentage of the crops.

stillborn
A baby that is born dead.

ADDITIONAL RESOURCES

SELECTED BIBLIOGRAPHY

Brown, Peter Harry and Pat H. Broeske. *Down at the End of Lonely Street: The Life and Death of Elvis Presley*. New York: Dutton, 1997. Print.

Keogh, Pamela Clark. *Elvis Presley: The Man. The Life. The Legend.* New York: Atria Books, 2004. Print.

Mason, Bobbie Ann. *Elvis Presley*. New York: Penguin, 2003. Print.

FURTHER READINGS

Edgers, Geoff. *Who Was Elvis Presley?* New York: Grosset & Dunlap, 2007.

Hampton, Wilborn. *Elvis Presley (Up Close)*. New York: Puffin Books, 2007.

Saddleback Educational Publishing. *Elvis Presley, Graphic Biography (Saddleback Graphic Biographies)*. Costa Mesa, California: Saddleback Educational, 2008.

WEB LINKS

To learn more about Elvis Presley, visit ABDO Publishing Company online at **www.abdopublishing.com**. Web sites about Elvis Presley are featured on our Book Links page. These links are routinely monitored and updated to provide the most current information available.

FOR MORE INFORMATION

For more information on this subject, contact or visit the following organizations.

Elvis's Birthplace
306 Elvis Presley Drive, Tupelo, MS 38801
662-841-1245
www.elvispresleybirthplace.com
Visitors can tour the home in Tupelo, Mississippi, where Elvis was born and spent his early years. An Elvis museum and gift shop are on the grounds as well.

Graceland
3765 Elvis Presley Boulevard, Memphis, TN 38116
800-238-2000
www.elvis.com/graceland
Fans can visit the infamous Graceland mansion that Elvis shared with friends and family. Rooms are maintained as they were lived in, and an audio-guided tour includes commentary and stories by Lisa Marie and even Presley himself.

Source Notes

Chapter 1. Shaking Up Variety Shows

1. Pamela Clark Keogh. *Elvis Presley: The Man. The Life. The Legend.* New York: Atria Books, 2004. Print. 3.

2. David Halberstam. *The Fifties*. New York: Random House, 1993. Print. 456.

Chapter 2. Born in a Shotgun Shack

1. "Tourism Info." *Visit Elvis Birthplace*. Elvis Presley Memorial Foundation of Tupelo, n.d. Web. 4 May 2012.

2. Alanna Nash. *Baby, Let's Play House: Elvis Presley and the Women Who Loved Him.* New York: HarperCollins, 2010. Print. 24.

3. Peter Harry Brown and Pat H. Broeske. *Down at the End of Lonely Street: The Life and Death of Elvis Presley*. New York: Dutton, 1997. Print. 13.

Chapter 3. Sun Studio Spark

1. Jon Garelick. "Sam Phillips: Rock's Visionary." *Sunrecordcompany.com*. Sun Record Company, n.d. Web. 17 Nov. 2011.

2. "Sun Rises On Rock." *CBS News*. CBS Interactive, n.d. Web. 4 May 2011.

3. Bobbie Ann Mason. *Elvis Presley*. New York: Penguin, 2003. Print. 24.

4. Ibid.

5. Glen Jeansonne, David Luhrssen, and Dan Sokolovic. *Elvis Presley, Reluctant Rebel: His Life and Our Times*. Santa Barbara: ABC-CLIO, 2011. Print. 38.

6. Peter Harry Brown and Pat H. Broeske. *Down at the End of Lonely Street: The Life and Death of Elvis Presley*. New York: Dutton, 1997. 34.

7. Pamela Clark Keogh. *Elvis Presley: The Man. The Life. The Legend.* New York: Atria Books, 2004. Print. 27.

8. "Why Elvis Presley Mattered, and Why He Still Matters." *Chicago Tribune* 3 Aug. 1997: 4. Print.

9. "Dixie Locke Emmons Talks About Elvis." *Elvis Australia: Official Elvis Presley Fan Club*. Elvis Presley Enterprises, 3 July 2009. Web. 4 Dec. 2011.

10. "Quotes by Elvis." *Elvis Presley: The Official Site of the King of Rock 'n' Roll*. Elvis Presley Enterprises, Inc., n.d. Web. 14 Nov. 2011.

11. Jerry Schilling. *Me and a Guy Named Elvis*. New York: Penguin Group, 2006. Print. 29.

12. "About the Opry." *Grand Ole Opry*. Grand Ole Opry, n.d. Web. 21 Feb. 2012.

13. "Horace Logan, 86; Coined Elvis Catchphrase." *New York Times*. New York Times Company, 16 Oct. 2002. Web. 4 May 2012.

Chapter 4. Colonel's Control

1. Bobbie Ann Mason. *Elvis Presley*. New York: Penguin, 2003. Print. 45.

2. Peter Harry Brown and Pat H. Broeske. *Down at the End of Lonely Street: The Life and Death of Elvis Presley*. New York: Dutton, 1997. Print. 59.

3. Bobbie Ann Mason. *Elvis Presley*. New York: Penguin, 2003. Print. 46.

4. "Million Dollar Quartet – Dec. 4 1956." *Sunrecords.com*. Sun Entertainment Corporation, 4 Dec. 2008. Web. 14 May 2012.

5. Patrick Humphries. *Elvis the #1 Hits: The Secret History of the Classics*. Kansas City, Missouri: Andrews McMeel, 2003. Print. 16.

6. "A Howling Hillbilly Success." *LIFE* 30 Apr. 1956: 64. Print.

Continued

Chapter 5. Elvis Fever Spreads

1. "Elvis Presley." *The Official Ed Sullivan Site*. SOFA Entertainment, n.d. Web. 14 Nov. 2011.

2. Bobbie Ann Mason. *Elvis Presley*. New York: Penguin, 2003. Print. 48.

3. "Elvis Presley on the Ed Sullivan Show 1957." *The Official Ed Sullivan Site*. SOFA Entertainment, n.d. Web. 7 Dec. 2011.

4. Pamela Clark Keogh. *Elvis Presley: The Man. The Life. The Legend.* New York: Atria Books, 2004. Print. 70.

5. Charles L. Ponce de Leon. *Fortunate Son: The Life of Elvis Presley*. New York: Hill and Wang, 2006. Print. 100.

Chapter 6. Presley Goes to Hollywood

None.

Chapter 7. Presley in the Army

1. Pamela Clark Keogh. *Elvis Presley: The Man. The Life. The Legend.* New York: Atria Books, 2004. Print. 98.

2. Ibid. 101.

3. Ibid. 118.

Chapter 8. Money, Movies, and Love

1. Pamela Clark Keogh. *Elvis Presley: The Man. The Life. The Legend.* New York: Atria Books, 2004. Print. 140.

2. Bobbie Ann Mason. *Elvis Presley*. New York: Penguin, 2003. Print. 103.

3. Ibid. 104.

4. Ibid.

5. Peter Harry Brown and Pat H. Broeske. *Down at the End of Lonely Street: The Life and Death of Elvis Presley.* New York: Dutton, 1997. Print. 335.

Chapter 9. Viva Las Vegas

1. Jerry Schilling. *Me and a Guy Named Elvis.* New York: Penguin Group, 2006. Print. 273.

2. Ibid. 233.

3. Ibid. 204.

4. Peter Harry Brown and Pat H. Broeske. *Down at the End of Lonely Street: The Life and Death of Elvis Presley.* New York: Dutton, 1997. Print. 355.

5. Pamela Clark Keogh. *Elvis Presley: The Man. The Life. The Legend.* New York: Atria Books, 2004. Print. 250.

6. Bobbie Ann Mason. *Elvis Presley.* New York: Penguin, 2003. Print. 162.

Chapter 10. The King Is Gone

1. "Quotes About Elvis." *Elvis Presley: The Official Site of the King of Rock 'n' Roll.* Elvis Presley Enterprises, Inc., n.d. Web. 20 Feb. 2012.

2. Susan Doll. *Elvis for Dummies.* New York: Wiley, 2009. Google Book Search. Web. 4 May 2012.

3. "Elvis Presley." *Rock and Roll Hall of Fame.* Rock and Roll Hall of Fame Museum, Inc., n.d. Web. 13 Dec. 2011.

4. Adrian Sainz. "Fans Flock to Graceland to Remember Elvis Presley." *ABC News.* ABC News Internet Ventures, 16 Aug. 2011. Web. 14 May 2012.

ABOUT THE AUTHOR

Stephanie Watson is a freelance writer based in Atlanta, Georgia. Over her 20-plus-year career, she has written for television, radio, the Web, and print. Watson has authored more than two dozen books, including *Celebrity Biographies: Daniel Radcliffe*, *Heath Ledger: Talented Actor*, and *Anderson Cooper: Profile of a TV Journalist.*

PHOTO CREDITS

Rex USA, cover, 3; Copyright Bettmann/Corbis/AP Images, 7, 49, 91, 96 (bottom); Everett Collection, 10, 13, 15, 33, 67, 76, 79, 95; STARSTOCK/Photoshot/Everett Collection, 19, 96 (top); Seth Poppel/Yearbook Library, 21; Carol M. Highsmith's America/Library of Congress, 23; Sun Records/Times Daily/AP Images, 25; AP Images, 29, 35, 37, 43, 59, 62, 64, 73, 82, 98 (bottom), 99 (top), 99 (bottom); Don Cravens/Time Life Pictures/Getty Images, 40, 97; NBC/NBCU Photo Bank/Getty Images, 45; 20th Century Fox Film Corp/Everett Collection, 51, 98 (top); MGM/AP Images, 53; Michael Ochs Archives/Getty Images, 57; skphotography/Shutterstock Images, 69; Keystone-France/Gamma-Keystone/Getty Images, 87; New York Daily News Archive/Getty Images, 89